HEM

(Holistic Enterprise Mechanization Process)

An agile approach to
analysis and design

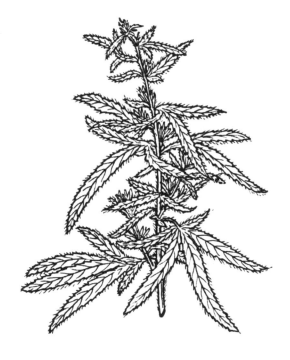

David E. Jones

ISBN-13: 978-1484184226

ISBN-10: 148418422X

Preface   1

   Audience   1

   About the Author   1

   About the Book   3

1. The Same Thing Every Night   6

   Requirements versus designs 6

   Why bother with requirements? 9

   Planning for failure and change 13

   Scaling complexity   14

   Agile methodologies   16

   Diagrams   18

2. The Story of HEMP   19

3. Gathering Requirements   25

   Business process story   27

   Requirement statement and idea to incorporate 30

   Actor definition and experience story 33

   Business case   36

   Writing and reviewing: the how 37

4. Building on Existing Systems   43

   Overlap description   44

   Gap description   45

5. User Interface Design   47

Screen outline   48

Wireframe and prototype   50

Screen flow and menu structure   51

Graphic design   52

Design review and testing   54

6. Technical Design   57

Data mapping and modeling   58

Data statement   60

Data model   62

Data mapping   63

Initial and test data   64

Automated process outline   65

System interface design   65

7. Implementation   67

Software development   67

Quality assurance   68

Business implementation   69

Packaged Software and Marketing   71

Ongoing Development   72

8. Tools and Systems   73

9. Case Studies   77

Requirement and design distinction   77

Analysis hysteria   79

Dive into design   81

HEMP ignited   84

Important Lessons   86

Appendix: Examples   **88**

Business process story   88

Actor definition   90

User experience story   90

Data statement   91

Data model   92

Screen outline   95

Wireframe   98

Screen data mapping   99

Useful web resources

Author's consulting web site:

http://www.DEJC.com

Author's LinkedIn profile:

http://www.linkedin.com/in/jonesde

Author's original open source ERP project Apache OFBiz aka The Open For Business Project:

http://ofbiz.apache.org

Author's new open source projects Moqui Framework and Mantle Business Artifacts:

http://www.moqui.org

Author's GitHub page:

https://github.com/jonesde

The HiveMind PM application mentioned in the book:

https://github.com/jonesde/HiveMind

Preface

Audience

HEMP is for people who create software, especially software used to automate and manage business operations and general activities that involve multiple people and systems. This includes those who play the roles of expert user, business analyst, user interface designer, system architect, software developer, and quality assurance technician.

Some principles and practices apply to building hardware and machines, but are really meant for effectively handling the complex processes and activities that are the domain of modern enterprise software.

About the Author

I started my career doing software development, soon getting into packaged and custom enterprise software. I founded The Open For Business Project (now Apache OFBiz) in 2001. OFBiz is an open source business automation suite (eCommerce, ERP, CRM, MRP, etc) designed for easy customization and used primarily for custom internal use systems and as a foundation for commercial derivative works.

In 2010 I started a series of open source projects that are the next generation of the ideas and patterns introduced in OFBiz. These projects include Moqui Framework and Mantle Business Artifacts which together are a foundation for a variety of implicitly integrated open source and commercial enterprise automation software.

These free software projects are funded mostly through consulting work to customize and extend them. Along the way I have consulted on around 120 projects, including involvement with around 20 from beginning to end and participating in every step along the way. While I have a technical background, from the beginning of my career it was painfully transparent how often technical solutions were requested and unsuccessfully attempted for solving business and management problems.

My meanderings in the world of analysis and design were pushed along by various projects with a total lack of analysts and designers involved, and by unclear, incorrect, and frequently changing designs that never did what the business users needed and wanted. Sometimes even worse was a myopic vision of an organization constrained by an existing system, making a separation of requirements and designs impossible.

The result of inadequate requirements and designs is predictable frustration for both business users and developers, budget and schedule overruns, and even cancelled or abandoned projects. After participating in many such projects, when I started to take the helm I knew something had to be done differently and that solutions from the traditional business analysis and software design world were complex and feckless.

The principles and practices described in this book are based on my consulting work, including a number of projects using HEMP itself. I originally put these ideas together and started using the term HEMP in 2007 while leading the analysis group in an OFBiz-focused consulting firm. HEMP has now contributed to the success of a number of custom software projects, and helped mitigate issues on others where it was applied either partially or late in the process.

About the Book

This book presents specific practices and tools for gathering and organizing requirements, producing designs based on requirements, developing software based on designs, and then making sure software implements the designs and the designs satisfy the requirements.

This book is a rewrite with improvements to HEMP as originally presented in the HEMP *light*, HEMP Complete, and HEMP Best Practices documents. While the general ideas are the same, recommendations about who should do what and how are slightly different.

Compared to the original documents, this book focuses more on business process stories and eliminates the recommendation to produce use case documents based on process stories (even on very large projects these have only limited utility). This book is also development tool and existing system agnostic so it does not mention OFBiz-specific development artifacts or practices as earlier works did.

The term "artifact" is used in this book in its broadest sense as something created by a human as part of analysis, design, and implementation efforts. An artifact may be a document, diagram, or machine readable information such as code and data.

While there are various tools and artifacts presented in this book, the primary artifact is the **business process story**. This artifact documents the actors and actions of every business activity and structures them around the progression from one activity to the next. Business process stories are created primarily by business analysts working with expert users, and are ultimately used by everyone involved with creating and using the software.

HEMP is about high quality results. So many software projects, especially in enterprise software, devolve into mediocrity as the people involved struggle to respond to what seems like constantly changing suggestions and demands from stakeholders.

With good engagement early in the process and efficient artifacts to facilitate effective communication this can be avoided. More than that, the experience can be satisfying for all involved as the result takes shape through collaboration in a quality form more comprehensive than the best and most complete anyone involved anticipated.

Whatever your role in a project, I recommend reading through the entire book and then refer to relevant chapters the first few times you work on each artifact.

If you get bogged down along the way read Chapter 9 (Case Studies) for a little motivation and perspective.

The book is designed to be consumable in a couple of hours and to be easily referenced later on when you need a reminder of how to do particular things and what to keep in mind as you do.

1. The Same Thing Every Night

The title of this chapter is from a comedy sketch by Bill Cosby about recurring patterns in family life around bedtime with a handful of children. Whether little or big, people come across familiar situations and tend to behave in consistent ways when we do. With good practices beatings can be avoided, at least if there is no one on the project who is "always poppings peoples" (this joke has more meaning after watching this Bill Cosby sketch, available on YouTube and elsewhere).

When building software systems, especially large and complex ones, it might seem like an evening of parents persuading their children to peacefully settle in for the night. Amidst the chaos some things are the same every time.

Requirements versus designs

This is the most important principle of HEMP. Making a clear distinction between business requirements and system designs will make the biggest difference of anything you might do to improve success of software and other development projects.

- Business requirements in their most basic form are business activities that fit into a process.
- A business activity is an actor performing an action. It is described by specifying **who** the actor is and **what** the actor does to perform an action.
- The position of a business activity within a process shows **when** the action is done.
- Designs communicate *how* a user representing the actor will perform the action and *where* in the system it will be done.
- Neither requirements nor designs should try to answer the "why" question.

> **Requirements** specify the **who, what**, and **when** whereas *designs* specify the *how* and *where*.

When writing requirements it is common to discuss business strategy and the costs and benefits of a variety of approaches to achieve business objectives. Ultimately these discussions need to end with a decision on <u>what</u> will be done, and that decision is all that needs to be documented for building a system.

Others involved may want to document the rationale behind these decisions, but that should be kept separate from requirement documentation. Including the why in requirements makes them very large, difficult to create and maintain, and is distracting or even confusing to designers and developers who will be working from these documents. If you want to document the *why* use a separate *business case* document to keep your requirements and designs as simple and clear as possible.

It might seem difficult to distinguish a business requirement from a system design, especially if you are mostly familiar with system designs labeled as requirements and have never seen a pure business requirement that is system agnostic (i.e. does not bias the design of the system).

> **Business requirements are about the business, not about the system. Designs are about the system.**

When writing business requirements it is well worth the effort to use whatever verbal acrobatics might be required to avoid describing the system to be built.

For example, instead of writing:

"When Customer submits order System sends Confirmation Email to Customer."

write:

"When Customer submits order Company automatically notifies Customer."

Writing *"Company automatically"* keeps the focus on what is done, and leaves the how to the design. Note that the second sentence also leaves out the detail of how Company will notify Customer. This avoids biasing the design, but if all involved are sure that email will be the only way this is done that detail may be included without really crossing the line into design.

Another example of a common business activity that is tempting to express in system terms is when a user enters data or views data from the system. We know this will be done with a computer system, but in business requirements it is helpful to describe the activity in a way that could lead to a pen and paper design just as well as a screen in an application.

Instead of writing:

"CSR types in Customer name, phone number, and address, and then submits the form."

simply write:

"CSR records Customer name, phone number, and address."

The principle to keep in mind is that business requirements should be limited to the business domain to make them an effective basis for design. The requirement information will then be flexible enough to facilitate creative and efficient design constrained only by actual needs of the organization.

Why bother with requirements?

The act of gathering and documenting business requirements in business terms helps engage users and sponsors of a project, and provides a clear direction to drive design and implementation efforts.

Engaging users and sponsors throughout the process improves alignment of the eventual system to the organization that will use it and sets the stage for satisfied acceptance, deployment, and long-term use of the new or improved system.

When working on designs without discussed and documented requirements different people are often thinking of different aspects of the business, sometimes different business activities altogether, and often a different understanding of who should be doing what and when.

> The typical experience of creating designs without requirements involves a number of people collaborating on design details with uncommunicated requirements in their heads.

The resulting designs are often poorly aligned with what the business needs. Getting to this false destination still involves long, frustrating discussions about details that seem irrelevant or nonsensical to others involved.

For business users driving the system design it is also easy to think a bad design is a good idea without considering who will be using it and what they will be trying to do.

> Designing software is difficult and trying to design "cold" (without requirements) is a setup for failure.

Even end-users who are very familiar with business activities often fail in cold-design efforts. Without a discussion of requirements that set the context and clarify the details needed for design, it is difficult to remember everything and easy to get hung up on design elements that won't be used and may be expensive to build.

> An initial focus on the business and documentation of business activities helps everyone involved to understand the business. Action-oriented business process stories provide a perspective on the business that is usually missed or glossed over in business plans and operating policy.

Writing process stories often involves uncovering details and prompting decisions that managers and executives have not addressed. The simple act of writing the story can tighten and clarify business operations, and involves a level of engagement and mutual understanding between those who run a business and those building software for it that is critical to the success and acceptance of the project.

In nonbusiness situations a similar pattern applies. Even consumer oriented software has sponsors and experts that drive the design.

Distinction between requirements and designs, and initial focus on business requirements is about building the right software and keeping everyone responsible engaged throughout the process.

What about "**analysis paralysis**" (endless cycles of analysis never leading to design or implementation) and "**failure to launch**" (project dies during analysis or design due to lack of confidence)? Effectively gathering, documenting, and organizing business requirements is the best way to get early traction in a project.

> Quality requirements are immediately actionable for design efforts. Quality designs are immediately actionable for implementation.

If a project stalls during requirements gathering or design it means the practices for gathering and artifacts for documenting them are poorly matched to the task at hand.

This is a common problem because so many analysts are trained on dozens of diagrams and document structures that require significant effort but have minimal utility. By using HEMP and a focus on business process stories you'll have the opposite experience: active engagement and actionable results.

What about business users and sponsors who refuse to engage or aren't capable of discussing the details needed to build a system? These are other symptoms of ineffective requirements gathering and documenting, or of skipping requirements and diving straight into designs. Business users and sponsors are often alienated early on by poor communication and a focus on details that have nothing to do with their day-to-day activities. The focus on business process stories keeps the early discussions in a domain they are comfortable with, and allows them to provide actionable details.

The greatest resistance to HEMP usually comes from:

- business analysts trained in other tools and practices
- developers who have had bad experiences with ineffective and frequently changing designs

Business users and sponsors who have been through failed projects may have light initial resistance, but quickly appreciate the early engagement and effective communication facilitated by business process story writing.

Starting with requirements consisting of business activities is a way to begin with the end in mind and produce a system that will meet the needs of the organization.

Eventually a system needs to be delivered. When it is delivered it will be subjected to the ultimate test of alignment with business activities: actual use.

Planning for failure and change

Software design and development are creative human efforts that stem from human strengths and are sensitive to human weaknesses. Some weaknesses are part of natural human tendencies, others are cultural, and others are learned as a side effect of education and other life experience. Unavoidable human weaknesses lead to failures during analysis, design, and implementation efforts.

The more complex a project the more human weaknesses make things difficult. It is difficult for users to express what they need, and even remember and articulate everything they do. The leap between what they do (business activities) and what software might look like to help them do it is difficult, but at least manageable as long as what they do is effectively documented.

Because it is easy to forget activities and not realize nuanced dependencies between activities, let alone create effective designs for those activities, changes are guaranteed during analysis, design, and development processes. Any methodology for these activities must be sufficiently adaptable to accommodate and minimize the impact of change.

On top of human weakness, business environments and goals change over time and it is critical that the software systems an organization uses be able to support changes within the organization and externally from partners, suppliers, and customers.

HEMP is a set of practices and artifacts for analysis and design that help keep changes earlier in the process where they require less effort to accommodate. This requires artifacts that are sufficient for capturing important details but simple enough for frequent change with minimal effort. The goal is the minimum effective set of artifacts, similar to the minimum effective dose principle in medicine. Beyond the minimum effective point come diminishing or negative returns.

This is the reason for the focus on simple artifacts like business process stories for documenting requirements, and avoiding artifacts like diagrams that are laborious to change during conversations and require supplementary documentation to be interpreted consistently by both business analysts and expert users who must create them and understand them to ensure they are correct and consistent.

Scaling complexity

Humans are not good at scaling complexity. We can only fit so much in our mental models of the world. As complexity increases the dependencies and interactions increase non-linearly, but even more significantly the human effort required to understand and automate the complexity goes up dramatically. The curve seems to be an approximation of x^2 so double complexity requires in four times the effort.

Necessary complexity can be managed by:

• refining and organizing requirements

- thorough design so implementation scales more linearly as complexity scales

Constraining complexity is easier to do during requirement analysis, especially when requirements are documented and organized according to business process.

Communication about business needs using requirements in the form of business activities makes it easier for expert users and other stakeholders to identify those that are more frequent and critical, and warrant more investment in automation. Communication about business needs using system designs makes it difficult for stakeholders to look at them in the context of the organization and evaluate their importance.

With requirements represented as business activities it is easy for stakeholders to understand the complexity they are requesting and give them a chance to simplify the business process or split activities into different phases to help prioritize and focus derivative efforts.

Trimming scope early (during requirements gathering) avoids unnecessary design and development effort which are expensive and time-consuming.

To effectively handle complexity in your project:

- write comprehensive and inclusive business process stories
- **review the stories and find ways to simplify and streamline business activities**
- make sure business process stories are easy to understand and well organized

- produce thorough, clear, and well organized system designs so they can be implemented literally
- review designs to make them as small and simple as possible while still meeting business requirements

Agile methodologies

Agile methodologies focus on development and rely on an external source for designs that drive the software development. A comprehensive agile approach including management, practices and tools adapts well to changing requirements and designs.

Agile methodologies prioritize frequent customer interaction and presenting results early and often. The biggest disconnect in the process is between requirements and design with a mix of both being presented to developers as a basis for their work. The customer is left on their own to make sure what they request of development is complete and will adequately satisfy organizational needs. The result is more difficulty for both customer and developer as they iterate toward what is hopefully a good result.

The solution is to help the customer by communication with expert users in language they are comfortable with, and that contains the details needed for design and development. With a focus on requirements the communication remains clear and to the point, providing a strong and flexible foundation for design and implementation.

The business process story and other HEMP artifacts can be used to drive a project that needs more predictive elements but the focus, as described in the last section, is on adaptability and works well feeding designs to a development team using agile methods.

This is especially true for larger projects (such as ERP projects) where a minimum set of business activities must be supported before the software is of use to an organization. The temptation with agile development methods is to neglect analysis and design, even analysis as simple as documenting the business activities that need to be supported. The result is difficulty predicting the overall size of the project.

> **HEMP shifts the focus toward analysis and design while remaining adaptive.**

To put HEMP in context it is similar to feature-driven development (FDD) with a focus on business activities and uses simplified artifacts to increase agility over the more complex and development oriented FDD. HEMP does not rely on object-oriented design and development and can be applied to a variety of architectures in existing systems and application development frameworks.

HEMP makes the most difference in automation of enterprise operations in any sort of organization where the business process involves interactions and hand-offs among a number of actors. Agile methods are best for projects involving incremental improvements but for these using HEMP will improve design and implementation system by basing them on requirements representing business activities and needs.

Diagrams

Humans have a natural instinct for language and even the verbally weakest of us can express and understand a wide variety of subtle ideas using language. Even so, it can be ambiguous and requires care in writing and review, with discussion among multiple people to be sufficiently clear and disambiguate subtle ideas. It also requires domain knowledge to anticipate common alternatives that people might consider and explicate which of them is desired.

Diagrams attempt to present a visual representation of ideas and disambiguate common ones with a variety of symbols. These symbol libraries are sometimes adequate for ideas of software structure and algorithms, but are rarely adequate for business ideas and the flow among the wide variety of activities necessary to operate organizations.

Diagrams are a sort of subset of language designed to represent specific ideas. They are low-resolution and without supporting text are often misunderstood.

Diagrams are cumbersome to maintain and keep consistent with supporting text and related artifacts, including other diagrams meant to represent different aspects of an idea or process.

The result is that diagrams are often not maintained during the high-paced changes that are natural when gathering requirements. On many projects where diagrams are used early on they are eventually abandoned while business process stories and other HEMP artifacts remain useful from analysis and design all the way through implementation and quality assurance.

2. The Story of HEMP

The Story of HEMP is a business process story just like the ones you will use to gather and organize requirements. It describes activities that make up HEMP in terms of the actors and actions. This story will give you an idea of what business process stories look like and introduce you to the business context that HEMP is designed for.

The bolded sentences are high-level activities made up of the more granular ones that follow. In large business process stories it is useful to create a summary story with just these high-level activities and links to the detailed stories that expand on them in separate documents.

Business Analyst and Expert User gather and document requirements. Expert User verbally describes business activities. Business Analyst documents activities in a business process story, asking questions as needed to clarify or expand on what Expert User described.

If Expert User describes a high-level idea and not a specific business activity then Business Analyst records it as an "Idea to Incorporate". If the idea is one that cannot be incorporated into the story then

Business Analyst records it as a requirement statement.

Once the basic structure of the process story is in place, Business Analyst and Expert User review the ideas to incorporate and make changes to the story, modifying each relevant activity and adding activities as needed to represent the idea throughout the business process.

For critical system users Business Analyst optionally works with Expert User and actual users representing specific actors to write user experience stories. Business Analyst reviews user experience stories to ensure each activity is included in the business process story.

Expert User or other stakeholders optionally write a business case document describing general business objectives and their financial impact. Business Analyst and Expert User review business process story against the business case details to ensure business objectives are achieved by the documented business activities.

Expert User reviews the story and comments on incorrect or unclear wording, additional relevant details, and anything else that comes to mind while reading the document. Business Analyst revises the business process story until Expert User is satisfied that everything relevant is represented and Business Analyst is satisfied that the story is understandable and actionable.

Business Analyst documents overlaps and gaps with an existing system. If there is an existing system that will be modified or extended, Business Analyst reviews each activity in the business process story and documents it as representing an overlap or gap in the existing system.

For each overlap Business Analyst documents how that activity is done in the existing system. For each gap Business Analyst documents any aspects of the existing system that are partial overlaps, and adds it to the list of gaps for design and implementation.

UI Designer designs screens and reports. Considering activities from the business process story and on gap descriptions (if available) UI Designer outlines the contents of screens and reports. UI Designer creates functional wireframes to accompany the screen and report outlines. UI Designer optionally creates screen flow diagram to show transitions between screens in each application.

Business Analyst reviews outlines and wireframes to verify the designs against the requirements. Business Analyst asks questions to UI Designer as needed, and may do the entire review in conversation with UI Designer.

UI Designer and Business Analyst review screen outlines and wireframes with Expert User by role playing. Expert User follows the business process story describing what they would do as each of the actors to perform each action. UI Designer plays the role of the system and describes how the system would respond to each user action, including changing from one wireframe to another as screens change.

UI Designer updates outlines and wireframes based on comments from Business Analyst and Expert User.

If comments from Expert User require business process changes Business Analyst updates relevant stories, and UI Designer updates design according to updated requirements.

System Architect models data and defines system interfaces. System Architect reviews each activity in business process stories and write data statements based on explicit or implied data to be recorded or reviewed by actors.

System Architect reviews screen and report outlines and maps each field to a field in the existing data model. If there is no adequate field in the existing data model, System Architect records data statements describing the field and its relationship to other data concepts.

System Architect reviews user interfaces and based on anticipated system architecture (especially for client applications on mobile or desktop devices) designs services and/or API for processing user input and preparing more complex data for presentation.

System Architect reviews business process story to identify all system-system interactions (as opposed to user-system interactions) and identifies an existing system interface for each, or defines a system interface (web service, file drop, API call, etc). System Architect maps each field in system interfaces to the data model. For fields without an existing field in the data model, System Architect records data statements describing the field and its relationship to other data concepts.

System Architect organizes data statements by data concept to group them for easier modeling and to remove redundant statements. System Architect maps each data statement to the data model and as needed extends data model based on data statements. System Architect updates user and system interface data mappings for relevant fields.

System Architect defines initial and test data to demonstrate how data is structured and to use for testing.

Software Developer implements user and system interface designs. Software Developer reviews business process story to understand the context of what needs to be built. Software Developer implements software described in user interface designs and technical designs.

System Architect, UI Designer, Business Analyst, and Expert User review implementation. System Architect reviews implementation to ensure that data comes from and goes to the fields described in data mapping. System Architect reviews service and/or API implementations and other system interfaces for consistency with the technical designs.

UI Designer reviews user interfaces and tests interactions against descriptions in the screen and report outlines, and layout against the wireframes.

Business Analyst reviews implementation by performing business activities described in the business process story. Business Analyst hands off each activity that is functionally supported to the Expert User for final review and testing.

If QA Technician is involved, QA Technician performs a comprehensive test of implementation against individual designs and end-to-end test based on the requirements in the business process story. QA Technician identifies and tests possible uses of the implementation that are not part of the business process story, and not an explicit part of the user and system interface designs.

With comprehensive testing done by QA Technician, other roles can reduce their efforts to spot review and testing, except for the Expert User who should review everything from a user perspective for acceptance of delivery.

This completes the story of HEMP. The activities described here tell you what to do (the requirements of HEMP), now we'll go over how to do them (the design of HEMP).

3. Gathering Requirements

Gathering requirements is the primary place where the business, or more generally the future users of the system, influence what the software needs to do and make sure that it supports all activities that are needed for the organization to operate.

Designs are always based on business activities, even if they are not articulated as requirements. This makes the leap to design without requirements difficult and error prone because different people involved may have different understandings of what the business does to operate, and may not realize it because discussions of designs are a poor way to communicate about business activities.

The first step for building a system to help an organization operate is gathering and documenting details about what the organization does to operate. These are the business activities documented in a business process story.

Other related artifacts that represent different perspectives of this big picture can be used to make sure that the process story is correct and complete.

These include actor definitions, user experience stories, and a business case document.

In rare cases there are requirements that don't fit well into the context of business activities, and these can be documented as requirement statements and used along with the business process story as the basis for the design of the system.

The requirements part of the process is the most important aspect of HEMP, and because of the nature of business activities and the people involved it is the least predictable and deterministic.

There are many different approaches and structures of documents and standards for diagrams that are used to try to do this. Having a large number of diagrams and documents in different forms makes the requirements gathering process difficult and often contributes to its failure or long-term stall in the all too common "analysis paralysis."

The artifacts used to do this in HEMP are the minimum effective set based on years of experience trying different artifacts and methodologies for gathering and documenting requirements. They include:

- business process story
- requirement statement
- idea to incorporate
- actor definition
- user experience story
- business case

These artifacts address all common concerns and perspectives that arise in analysis efforts and provide a place for everything along with structure to keep them organized.

With that context in mind, let's get started with the most important requirements document, and the primary one used to drive design efforts: the business process story.

Business process story

A business process story describes what an organization does to operate. It is written from the perspective of the organization and not of any individual actor, like a user experience story is.

It is natural that business processes transition from actor to actor. Managing hand-off between actors is an important aspect of what enterprise automation systems do. This is critical information to represent in business requirements. Including all actors in one flow is the easiest way to do this. Business process stories naturally handle the flow between actors by naming the actor in each activity.

> Each sentence in a business process story represents a business activity.

Each sentence should be structured as an active verb phrase with an action and the actor who performs the action. The opposite of an active verb phrases is a passive one where the actor is not identified. All passive sentences in a story should be changed to clearly identify the actor.

An example of a passive sentence with the actor omitted is:

"The picklist barcode is scanned."

To rephrase that in an active voice and specify the actor use:

"Packer scans the picklist barcode."

Just as in traditional use cases an actor may be a person or a separate system. The system being built or customized should not be mentioned to avoid biasing the design that will be based on these requirements. The goal of a business process story is to be a pure requirement and not cross the line into design territory. Going back to the "Requirements versus designs" section in chapter 1, this means describing what each actor does, but not how the actor does it. That is part of the design.

When something needs to be triggered automatically one way to avoid mentioning the system to be built is to write something like "Company automatically ..." instead of "System ...."

Another thing to avoid in a story is describing **why** a business activity is done. This is important information for those specifying requirements, and is often a topic of conversation while writing stories and deciding what should be done, but it should not be included in the business process story. An effective place for "why" ideas if you want to record them is a separate business case document linked to from the relevant parts of a story. In a story they add bulk that makes maintenance more difficult and irrelevant detail that makes it more difficult to pick out details important during design and implementation.

One thing to include in a story is conditional statements and alternate flows. Business operations are complex by nature, especially when business innovates to provide better offerings at lower prices, or to better serve stakeholders and customers.

Alternate flows should stay close to the primary flow they branch from. The words that distinguish the alternative should be at the beginning of the first sentence in the paragraph for the alternate flow. This makes it easier to identify that a paragraph represents an alternate flow and not the next step in the primary flow. When going back to the main flow it is helpful to start the paragraph with a phrase that refers to the last point in the primary flow or how to make the decision to continue based on completion of one or more branches in the flow.

How much detail should be included in a business process story? The level of detail can extend to listing fields recorded or reviewed by an actor. If the detail goes much beyond that it is best to put it in a **supporting document** linked to from the story. Some common supporting documents include:

- specifications for communication with other systems (system actors in the story)
- example reports and printed documents
- existing paper or other forms
- lists of fields along with definitions and constraints

The result of story writing efforts is a document that describes what the business does in sufficient detail to provide what a designer needs and in a structure that makes the information readily available while designing for each user or system interaction. A business process story includes more detail than general requirements statements and inherently structures those details to help ensure they are considered during design.

Requirement statement and idea to incorporate

When writing stories it is common for ideas to come up that don't easily fit in the story, but need to be represented somehow.

These ideas are usually business rules or objectives that don't represent an activity. Most are crosscutting concerns that influence a number of activities and can be represented in the business process story by making sure they are covered in each relevant activity. In other words they are high-level ideas that need to be broken down and detailed in the context of each relevant business activity to make the requirements more useful for design and implementation.

An example of such a business rule is:

"All user-entered postal addresses will be validated by an online service and the user allowed to select the corrected or originally entered address."

This should be broken down to describe the particular steps involved, and those steps should be mentioned with all relevant activities, in this case all activities that involve recording a postal address. One story section might look like:

"Customer creates new profile. Customer enters postal address information including: address line, optional unit number, city, state and postal code. Company

automatically sends address to USPS online address validation service. USPS returns a corrected address or error message if no matching valid address is found. Company presents corrected address or error message to Customer. If there is no error Customer reviews corrected and original addresses and records which one to use. If there is an error Customer may edit the address (going back to the address entry activity) or use the entered postal address as-is."

When an idea can be broken down in this way and covered in all relevant activities it is an **idea to incorporate** into the business process story. These may come up while writing stories and interrupt the flow of thought and conversation. It is best to make a note about the idea in an "Ideas to Incorporate" section (or separate document) and then move the conversation back to the story flow. Go back later and incorporate each idea into the story by breaking it down in the activities affected by it.

People are good at thinking of activities as a sequence of events. Capturing this flow of thought in story form is a good way to leverage this strength. When thinking in a flow people remember more and leave out less than they would discussing general ideas without context and process.

This is one reason for the focus on process stories and not on requirement statements. The other main reason is that when designing a system having details in order of sequence of activities is far more useful than activities or general statements structured in any other way.

However, some ideas are not crosscutting concerns that can be incorporated into a process story and need to be tracked separately, or are most easily documented separately.

> **One common type of idea to document separately is a system design constraint that needs to be documented but shouldn't be part of a business process story.**

Business rules are a useful tool for expressing general requirements, and there is much good literature about gathering requirements as business rules. To be more easily actionable business rules should be broken down across relevant business activities and then designs based on those. Just like general ideas described above some business rules are best broken down and incorporated into process stories this way, and others are cumbersome to break down and should be listed along with general requirement statements. If a set of rules applies to a single activity record it in a supporting document linked to from that activity in the story.

Localization in a specific set of languages is an example of this when any actor may interact with the system in any of the languages. If only certain actors or only certain activities will involve use of a specific language then it is best tracked as part of actor descriptions or as a constraint within the business process story.

Another example of a crosscutting concern is storing credit card numbers in a separate system. There are a variety of activities involving both human and independent system actors that need to be added to different points in the business process story to cover this idea. In this example those would include a customer or CSR recording credit card information, the company requesting payment authorization from the payment gateway, and so on.

Actor definition and experience story

An actor definition describes the nature of the actor (person, system, etc) and its primary roles and responsibilities. The description should include overlaps and distinctions between this and other actors.

An actor definition may summarize high-level activities or processes the actor is responsible for but should not try to include all activities for the actor. For critical actors, or specific processes that are most significant for the actor, you may want a narrative from the perspective of that actor and that is done with a user experience story.

A user experience story is a sort of "day in the life of" narration. The purpose is to make sure that actor's activities and concerns are represented in a way that is easiest to review by someone who plays the role of that actor or is familiar with the system representing the actor. By focusing on a single actor it is easier to make sure that everything the actor does is documented.

This story is less formal than the business process story and because it is about what a single actor does there is no need to identify the actor for every activity. It is also more permissible to include some design elements in user experience stories with ideas about the system eventually being built. This should still be minimized as the purpose is to gather requirements and not to design the system.

A user experience story can be used to clarify requirements, but should not be the basis of a design. All activities and relevant details from a user experience story should be incorporated into the business process story.

In a way the user experience story is a crosscutting concern like the idea to incorporate concept described in the previous section. It is a focus on a certain aspect of the business that is easier to work with, but should be incorporated into the main business process stories to put the actor's activities in context and make effective design easier.

Some processes may seem to involve only a single actor, but it is rarely really the case. For example a customer placing an order on an eCommerce web site is just the customer actor interacting with the system to be built. Even in this case the organization automatically does various things and there are other actors such as payment processing, tax calculation, and shipping charge estimation systems that are involved in the process.

An even better way to write the story of a customer placing an order is to write it more generally and not cross the line into design at all. In other words, you wouldn't write the story of a customer placing an order on an eCommerce web site, you just write the story of a customer placing an order.

An eCommerce web site is one design to accommodate this business process, but there may be others such as placing an order over the phone with a customer service rep or by mail with a paper form. If these are very different processes they should be different stories, but if they are similar in the organization a single story will do, with alternate flows for the customer communication with a CSR and so on.

Writing a user experience story for the customer is a great way to start this process, and you'll have multiple user experience stories for a customer placing an order through different means. Once these are written you can more easily decide how to organize them before you start incorporating the user stories into the business process story.

This way of writing and using user experience stories is different from user stories and use cases that describe what the user does and how the system works in literal terms so that it can be used directly for software development efforts.

The reason using them that way is not recommended in HEMP is that it does not separate business requirements and system designs. For all the reasons why this is important see the "Requirements versus designs" section in chapter 1.

In HEMP the screen outline is similar in purpose to these user stories and use cases, though different in that screen outlines are designs based on requirements found in the business process story so descriptions of activities and context for them are separate.

Business case

A business case includes details about organizational objectives and their impact on revenue and expenses. The purpose of the document is to explain rationale behind decisions about activities in business process stories and help prioritize activities based on objectives and financial impact (if applicable).

The document should be structured around general objectives of the organization with more detailed objectives broken down under each. This is a different structure than the business process story because it has a different purpose and the information in it has a different natural structure. Links in each document to relevant sections in the other should be used to correlate between them.

In some organizations documents like this will already exist. They can be used as a starting point for the business case document, or if they are sufficiently close to what is described here they may be usable as-is. Whether existing documents are used or a new document is written it should be done in collaboration with executives of the organization and reviewed and approved by them.

> The information in this document should not include sensitive data such as budgets and expected ROI for the project. Everyone involved with the project will see this document.

This document can be based on a business case used for funding, but with confidential details removed. It is similar in content but different in purpose.

Writing and reviewing: the how

The focus of this chapter so far has been what these artifacts are meant for and guidelines for how to structure them and constraints to make sure they stay close to their purpose. The major missing piece is how you go about gathering the information and documenting it using these artifacts.

The highest level artifact is the business case document. This document is not necessary, but if it will be used it should be written first, or at least started immediately as progress begins on other artifacts. In order for organizational objectives and priorities to be most effectively represented the business process story and other artifacts need to be written with them in mind. The process story can be modified with some level of effectiveness to accommodate these objectives and priorities after they are written, but the result is better if they are understood and considered all along the way.

In theory an expert user, or a group of expert users, can write a business process story for an analyst to review before handing it over for design. In practice this doesn't work very well. Some people take to process story writing quickly and effectively, but most people have a hard time with it.

Writing a business process story is best done by someone with experience doing it, and someone who understands the business domain and relevant business systems well enough to understand the difference between what is done and how it is done, and focus on what is done.

For these reasons it works best if the expert user, or group of expert users, describes what the business does to operate and a business analyst records this as actor and action descriptions in a business process story. This approach also allows the business analyst to feedback what they understand in a form that is easy for all to understand, helping everyone involved to better communicate and have more confidence that the communication is successful.

Writing the process story for an organization is easiest to do by starting with a single high-level story that covers the entire scope of operations. If there is a single person who understands most of what the business does they can provide the information for this story. In most larger organizations this will require a team of people that are responsible for different parts of the business.

Once a high-level story is in place a business analyst can work with one or more representatives from each group in the organization to flesh out the details for the parts of the process they are responsible for or work with most.

To separate parts of the process into other documents as the story grows: write a single sentence representing a high-level activity, put that sentence in the high-level story, create a new story document with that sentence as its title, and add details to that new story document. Here are some examples of high-level activity sentences:

- *Warehouse fulfills sales order.*
- *Business Analyst and Expert User gather and document business requirements.*

- *Inventory Manager places purchase order.*
- *Project team plans upcoming sprint.*

The level of detail needed in each detailed process story before design begins should enough that user and system interfaces can be designed from them. This means that information to be recorded or reviewed should be enumerated and the activities should be granular enough that they can be the basis of specific interactions with the system.

Enumerating information in most cases means literally listing fields that the actor will record or review (i.e. fields that the system will take as inputs and return as outputs). To avoid biasing design use verbs like "record" and "review" instead of verbs like "submit", "enter", and "display", that are system-specific terms.

If there is much field, rule or other detail for a certain activity or set of activities instead of cluttering the story with it put it in a separate **supporting document** and link to it from the story.

Getting to this level of detail will require the analyst to think of eventually building a system, even if that system and how the actor performs each action should not be included in the process story.

The high-level story will provide structure for most activities within an organization where the completion of one activity naturally leads to the next, but there are many that don't happen as part of a single high-level flow. The main category of these is activities that are triggered on periods of time. Instead of incorporating these into the main process flow it is easier to organize and maintain time-based events in a time flow structured around fiscal and/or calendar time periods (years, months, weeks, quarters, seasons, etc).

When writing the process story the business analyst will need to ask various questions to **get sufficient detail** and to **explore possible alternatives** for activities that achieve a business goal. This is where a good business analyst adds value and why it is important for the business analyst to understand both the business domain being documented and how systems in that domain usually work.

If a base system to customize has already been chosen it is helpful if the business analyst is familiar with that system, or if someone familiar with it is present when writing the process stories. While the process stories should not include system and design details, a person familiar with the capabilities of the existing system can comment on whether each activity is supported in the system and recommend alternatives that would be at least partially supported to save effort later on.

Throughout the story writing process ideas will come up that are important but don't fit into the current process flow being discussed, or that are relevant to the flow but apply to many other parts of the stories as well. These are the "ideas to incorporate" mentioned above. To avoid interrupting the natural flow of the discussion: record these in a separate section of the document, write about any activities that apply to the current story section you are working on, and then go back to these ideas to incorporate them later on.

In many cases one reason to do this is that other expert users and stakeholders need to be involved with the discussion so scheduling a separate meeting would be necessary. Either way, they often change the context of the discussion and more time and effort is required to get back into the flow, with increased chances that something is missed as people switch back and forth.

If an idea comes up that does not fit naturally in a business activity, or is time based instead of fitting into the current flow, briefly add those to the documents they belong in and move back to the current process flow. The business analyst may be able to do this without interrupting or derailing the discussion.

Once a first draft of a business process story is complete you can review and refine it with a different perspective by defining each actor mentioned in the process story, and optionally write user experience stories for actors with more complex or important involvement with the organization.

This is often a good idea for customers and other actors external to the organization because they use the system infrequently and their interactions are sensitive and critical to meeting organizational objectives. Other types of actors to consider are heavy users of the system and those that have complex responsibilities spread across different parts of the overall business process.

Defining actors mentioned in the process story is a useful exercise in identifying similarities and distinctions between them. A result of this effort is often redefining, merging, and splitting actors. As this is done make sure to update all the process stories for each actor change. While doing this also review the process stories to make sure actors are consistently referred to by the same name.

As user experience stories are completed review each business activity mentioned in them and make sure it is represented completely in the business process story. Also make sure that the sequence of activities is consistent between the user experience story and the business process story. Other refinements to the business process story may come from this effort, but these two are the main objective for it.

If a business case document is used it should be considered throughout the effort of writing both user experience and business process stories. At this point it is also a good idea to review the planned activities in the business process story against the business case to make sure that objectives are addressed and that priorities are identified (usually as comments inline within the story).

Once the stories are in a final draft review them with other stakeholders including organization executives, general system users, UI designers, system architects, and developers. A business analyst should make changes to the stories based on comments from these other stakeholders. Changes based on feedback are not the only reason to do this. It is also critical for early business engagement, eventual acceptance, and successful deployment and use of the system.

If a formal approval of requirements is desired by the organization before design begins that should be done at this point by the person or people with this responsibility. Then it's time for design to begin... almost.

4. Building on Existing Systems

Whether building a system from the data model up or extending a fully functional existing system good requirements are necessary. From there paths diverge depending on the strategy for reuse.

If you are building from scratch the next step after gathering and documenting requirements is to create user and technical level designs.

If you are extending or customizing an existing system and plan to reuse as much of it as possible, from the user interface down, then do a gap/overlap analysis between the business process story and the surface functionality of the system to provide documentation for existing functionality (overlaps) and identification of functionality that needs to be built (gaps).

If you are customizing a system with the strategy of a completely custom user interface but reuse of lower-level parts of the system such as logic and data structures then do a gap/overlap analysis between the business process story and these lower-level parts of the system to produce technical documentation on artifacts that should be reused, and identification of requirements that will require artifacts to be built. In this case there is an intentional 100% gap for the user interface, so it will be a major part of the design effort.

A gap/overlap analysis effort is a simple process of going through each activity in the business process story, researching existing functionality for that business activity, and then documenting the results. Some activities won't involve any system interaction and the result will be a simple statement why this is the case.

Overlap description

For activities that appear to be fully supported by the existing system (a 100% overlap) write an overlap description. An overlap description may cover a series of activities from the process, so references to the relevant activities from the business process story is the first part of this document.

For each activity referenced in the overlap description add a reference (or link) from the business process story. Once all activities have been reviewed for gaps and overlaps the business process story will be an overview of what is supported in the existing system and what is not.

The rest of the document is a set of instructions describing how the activities are done using the system. This should be detailed enough that an end-user could follow the instructions having never seen the system before. If it is helpful include UI screenshots or API/service references in the relevant part of the instructions.

An overlap description can be the basis for end-user documentation, but the first use of it will be a thorough review with expert users to validate that it is really an overlap. If the overlap is approved by expert users there is no need for design and development work for the associated activities.

If issues are found with the overlap but those issues are satisfied by some other part of the existing system or some other way of using it the issues may be addressed by modifying overlap description.

If issues are found that are really not supported by the existing system then change the overlap description to a **partial overlap description**. At the point where a business activity cannot be done in the system describe the gap, but leave the rest of the document as-is.

A partial overlap document should be used when activities are mostly supported and only minor changes need to be made. If there is no functionality for the requirement or major changes will be needed the structure of a gap description will be more useful.

Gap description

When customizing an existing system total gaps are usually limited to activities that are unique to a particular industry or way of operating an organization and not likely to be supported by a more generic system. In this circumstance a number of activities in a sequence may not be supported and should be combined in a single gap description.

When an activity is not supported but some functionality or at least data model elements exist that are useful for the activity there is a partial gap for that activity.

The overall structure of a gap description is a list of the business activities not supported in the system with an optional sub-list of relevant artifacts in the existing system that should be considered in the design and implementation.

Just as with the overlap description link to the gap description from the business process story for each activity represented by the gap.

Once gaps and partial overlaps are identified and referenced in the business process story, design and development can be focused on them.

5. User Interface Design

The primary purposes of user interface design are:

- show **how** activities from business process stories involving human actors will be done
- represent the UI in a way that expert users, other prospective users, and stakeholders can understand and validate it
- provide information to developers to build what is intended by designers and understood by users

The aspects of a user interface are the functional and the visual (graphic). Most of what is specified in each is independent of the other, but eventually the functional and graphic designs must come together for the development of the UI.

The most basic artifact describing a functional UI design is a screen outline. This simple document is organized by areas of the screen and describes each label, form, image, etc and the user interactions and system responses applicable to each.

To complement the screen outline a functional wireframe visually shows the layout of each screen. Details mainly live in the screen outline as the descriptive text that the diagram is based on, but you can help communicate how the screen should function with multiple wireframes showing different screen states and description bubbles on the wireframe.

If implementation tools used for the project include a rapid prototyping ability these can be used for partly functional prototypes instead of wireframes.

As screens are designed it is helpful to document the flow between screens in the application using a screen flow diagram. Where applicable also specify where they go in a menu structure outline.

The visual or graphic design can start out as a style guide independent of the functional design. As screen designs are finalized all or selected screens can be worked up using the style guide to produce images that demonstrate the applied graphic design.

Each part of the design should be reviewed and "tested" by expert users and as needed by other prospective users as well, especially for screens designed for users such as customers that will use them infrequently and without training.

Screen outline

The structure of a screen outline should verbally mirror the visual structure of a screen. Beginning with a text screen outline makes it easier to brainstorm and move things around as the design takes shape.

Rough wireframes showing sections of the screen might be useful for more complicated screens, but avoid showing too much detail, like actual form fields and such, until the outline is mostly complete. When you do get to the functional wireframes or prototypes changes may be needed, but they should be fewer and simpler if the general idea of the screen has been thought through in advance and documented in a screen outline.

Under the top level outline items (representing screen sections) you'll have a list of what goes in each section. This would include labels, images, links, buttons, forms, data tables, and so on.

Under each of these screen elements include details about what is displayed, the user interactions possible, and in general terms what the system does when the user interacts with it (including changes to the screen or references to another screen displayed after).

The screen outline should be primarily functional and leave out visual and graphic elements except to reference elements defined in the style guide such as heading levels, logo variations, different classes of text, and so on. Actual fonts, sizes, colors, and other visual aspects should be left to the style guide.

To avoid redundancy write separate outlines for shared sections of screens like headers, footers, menus, and side bars. If the application is structured in a hierarchy, usually mirroring the **menu structure**, then outline that structure separately and reference shared elements in it that are used at each level of the hierarchy. For example reference headers at the top level, tab-set names above the tabs listed in the hierarchy, etc.

Just like in gap and overlap descriptions each element in screen outlines should link to the activities in the business process story they are based on. Also add reverse links from the business process story to the screen outlines sections for easier future reference and to make it easier to keep screens updated as stories change and stories updated if a business activity is changed or clarified.

Wireframe and prototype

A functional wireframe represents the layout of a screen in a way that is difficult with only text in a screen outline. The two are complementary.

For screens with a simple layout a wireframe may not be necessary because the details in the screen outline are sufficient. The opposite is not true, a wireframe without a screen outline doesn't have enough information to be understood alone; it needs the details in the screen outline.

Some people think more visually than verbally so wireframes are easier to understand. If you are having trouble with key stakeholders or expert users not reading the screen outlines, similar details can be included in wireframes using comment bubbles and various wireframes for the same screen showing how it looks as each activity in the corresponding business process story is done.

Another purpose for wireframes is to use as a visual aid when role playing to review and "test" a user interface design. For this reason you may want to create wireframes for all screens, even the screens with a simple layout. Also for this reason you may need wireframes for screens in different states to match the activities in the business process story that will be used to evaluate the design.

There are many tools for creating wireframes, and almost any will do. A whiteboard or paper can even work well, just take a picture of them to create a digital copy that is easier to share and store along with other artifacts.

If the tools you are using to build the actual software provide a way to quickly create screens these work well as wireframes and may give you a head start on development. One downside to this approach is that user interface designers may have a hard time using the tools. It is common to go through multiple rounds of design and make many changes to wireframes during the process, so the UI designer needs to be able to modify them easily.

Screen flow and menu structure

As the number of screens in an application and system grows it is difficult to keep track of how they all fit together without a little help.

A screen flow diagram shows how the user moves from one screen to another as they interact with each. Each screen is a node in the diagram and lines going out of the screen represent transitions triggered by links, buttons, form submissions, and so on.

A transition represents a move from one screen to another and may also represent logic executed along the way. When the target screen is selected based on the results of that logic add a decision node along the transition line with the various targets splitting from it.

Each screen node should have the name of the screen, and each transition between nodes a short name based on either what the user did to trigger the transition or on what is done when that transition is followed.

All the information in the screen flow diagram comes from the screen outlines but is somewhat buried in the text making it more difficult to see how the user moves between screens, all the ways a user can get to a screen, and all the possible targets when transitioning out of a screen.

For larger systems split the diagram into one per application. Transitions between screens that cross applications can go to a simple label representing an external reference to the target screen instead of trying to directly include all diagrams in a large one.

Graphic design

Graphic design can add flavor, comfort, and even excitement to a software application. Good graphic design gives users a feeling that they are working with quality software, regardless of whether true.

It is similar to signals of quality in automobiles like low noise and perceptible vibration, and recognizable quality materials in trim and finish. Low noise and vibration don't necessarily mean the underlying frame and engine components are high quality, and are engineered separately and implemented with additional hardware. Still, the user perception is the same and very important for the vehicle to be perceived as high quality.

Graphic design also communicates to users what they should expect from an application and what sort of organization it represents. This is true for internal users but most important for external ones.

As important as graphic design is, it should not be mistaken for functional design and good graphic design paired with poor functional design will come across transparently shallow. Don't have graphic design headline the show, even if the organization is in a fashionable vertical. Also don't have artists or graphic design focused firms work on functional design. It is important that experts in each realm work together to produce the necessary complementary aspects of a high quality result.

The most basic part of the graphic design is a style guide. If an organization already has one it can be used. If one does not yet exist at least a basic one should be created to document colors, font faces and sizes, logos and other images, and so on.

Along with the normal elements of a style guide for building software include other information such as white space guidelines, shapes and colors for borders, look of buttons and links and form fields, and other common elements of screens.

Once these general graphic design elements are in place and at least some early functional wireframes are available the application of the style guide can be demonstrated with mockups based on both. Mockups show the applied graphic design and should be reviewed along with the general style guide to make sure relevant stakeholders understand just how things will look once the user interface is implemented.

Design review and testing

Creative genius for both functional and graphic designers is necessary for a good design, but not sufficient. Expert users and others who participate in requirements and designs naturally review them as part of the process, and important stakeholders should be explicitly included in this. In addition it is helpful to have prospective end users review and "test" the designs.

When reviewing and testing designs keep the intended use in mind. Will each application be used by people trained to use it and who use it frequently? If so don't focus on first impressions, dig in a little more and focus on how efficiently they can perform business activities. Will each application be used by people who are not trained and will use it infrequently? If so first impressions and cold use are important and should be thoroughly tested.

The most common form of user testing is done when applications, or at least functional prototypes of them, are complete and usable. Tools such as eye tracking and video recording of both user and screen offer a good understanding of how people understand and respond to user interfaces. These are mostly useful for evaluating first impressions and cold (untrained) use and are important for public-facing applications and web sites. While these can be done in-house hiring one of the many good specialized firms is a good idea as they not only offer equipment and experience but also a fresh point of view.

The downsides to this form of user testing are that it is only really possible late in the design and development process, and it leads to unhelpful and even counterproductive feedback for applications where users are trained and will use them frequently.

To get some design feedback early on use role playing with visual aids such as wireframes or semi-functional prototypes. A UI designer plays the role of the system and holds the wireframe or controls the prototype. A user, starting with an expert user and later moving to other prospective users, plays their role and a verbal interchange ensues. It is good to have a third party observe and take notes as the people playing roles will be focused on other things.

The user describes what they do (without prompting) to use the UI design to accomplish business activities documented in business process stories. The UI designer playing the role of the system responds verbally with how the system responds to the user action. Both refer to wireframes and other visual aids as needed to make the communication easier and more clear.

If the application being tested is one where training and frequent use is expected, the UI designer should begin with a summary of how the system is intended to be used. If end-user documentation has been written or if overlap descriptions are available use them as applicable. After training go through a few rounds of role playing before asking the user for comments or having a third party write an evaluation of the application.

During review and testing of the design changes to the design are likely and should be done across all design artifacts being used (screen outline, wireframes, screen flow and menus, and graphical design).

Some issues may come up involving inadequate or incorrect requirements. In these cases begin by updating requirements in business process stories and if applicable user experience stories, actor definitions, and requirement statements. Once those are updated make corresponding changes to the UI design artifacts.

Whatever the nature of the change don't just discuss it and move on, be sure to go back through the review and testing process again for changed screens and related screens as needed.

Once designs are completed the work of the UI designer is done and the work transitions to architects and developers, starting with technical design.

6. Technical Design

A good technical design is the first step to high quality and efficient implementation. It allows more senior system architects and developers to guide the course of implementation without doing all the development work themselves.

After years of trying both I still believe that the ideal way to develop software is with a small group of expert developers, but this approach is rarely chosen or feasible in the real world for a variety of real and imagined reasons. The reality is that most development is outsourced and off-shored, and often to people who are adequately knowledgeable and capable but with little experience relevant to the current project and, if applicable, existing systems. Splitting work this way is also helpful for training and mentoring less experienced developers.

Dividing labor does cause some inefficiency because it takes time for the architect or senior developer to write up technical designs with enough detail for the developer to understand, and it takes time for the developer to work through those details (duplicating knowledge already in the architect's head), and time for both to discuss details and make sure they are communicated and understood correctly.

It is more difficult for architects and senior developers to work with technical details at this level and get everything correct when they are not writing the actual code. The process of coding is where the rubber hits the road and vagueness surfaces. Even the best architects and senior developers miss details when working at this level. This isn't ultimately an issue as developers writing code will run into problems and need to resolve them with the architect. While it is more difficult and inefficient, it does get multiple people looking at the same details and that helps vet and improve them.

The HEMP technical design artifacts include:

• data statement
• data model
• data mapping
• initial and test data
• automated process outline
• system interface design

The artifacts in this chapter are designed to represent the most important information for a consistent and high quality implementation without excessive busywork or redundancy (which is the foundation of inconsistency).

Data mapping and modeling

Whatever happens during the day at the end of the day all that matters is data and what that data means. On a larger time scale systems and business processes change. On a smaller time scale transactions begin and end, only lasting a short time. What remains between across all of this is data.

The structure and meaning of data, be it in a relational, object, or other model, determines much of the structure and function of application code. Code and related implementation artifacts are in essence a representation of the meaning of the data they work with.

If a data model is clean, and the meanings of model elements are used consistently, the entire system from user and system interfaces to automated processes and reports will be cleaner, easier to write, and less costly to maintain.

If you are using a data model from an existing system your options are limited for improving it, and even if it is not ideal it is better to reuse it as much as possible rather than creating redundant data structures.

If you are building a system from scratch the idea of a universal data model may be helpful. This idea has been around for a while and a logical universal data model was developed by a few people and refined and published by Len Silverston in his 3 volume series <u>The Data Model Resource Book, Revised Edition</u>. The physical data models in the open source ERP projects I have worked on are based in this logical universal data model, and it is also used in a number of custom systems in organizations small and large around the world.

When building or extending a data model these logical elements are useful. They are normalized for minimal redundancy and map cleanly to real world business concepts. This makes them easy to map to the data elements described (or implied) in business process stories and other requirements.

Data statement

Data statements are an artifact to bridge the gap between abstract data concepts described or implied in requirements and a physical data model.

The idea of a data statement comes from Object Role Modeling (the other ORM), a conceptual data modeling methodology by Dr. Terry Halpin. For more information see http://www.orm.net.

Each data statement is a sentence easily understandable by technical and nontechnical stakeholders. To be meaningful and easily mappable to a physical data model, data statements need to follow a specific structure. ORM includes a way to diagram data statements, but it is often easier to work with a large number of them in plain text form.

A data statement sentence always has a subject, verb, and object. Any verb can be used as long as it describes the relationship between the subject and object. The subjects and objects are data concepts that could eventually be tables, columns, classes, entities, fields, etc. When initially writing data statements don't worry about that, just document the data relationships and then decide on the physical representation based on them.

Some verbs you will use a lot include "has", "uses", "is", and "consists of", but again you can use any verb that describes how the data concepts relate. Some examples of data statements include:

- Person is a Party.
- Organization is a Party.
- Party has zero to many Contact Mechanisms.

- Postal Address is a Contact Mechanism.
- Telecom Number is a Contact Mechanism.
- Postal Address has one or more address lines.
- Postal Address has a city.
- Postal Address optionally has a country.
- Postal Address has a postal code.

These data statements are a partial set of statements describing the Party and Contact Mechanism logical data models from <u>The Data Model Resource Book</u> mentioned earlier.

The data concepts for data statements come from requirements, mostly the business process story. Any activity where an actor records or reviews information is an explicit description of one or more data concepts. Many data concepts come from things implied by activities and require a small mental leap to identify. The general idea is simple: write data statements for every bit if information that needs to be recorded or reviewed as part of each activity.

Initially organize data statements by the flow of the business process story. Once that is done reorganize the data statements to group them by data concepts, especially higher level concepts that will become tables, entities, or classes.

With the statements organized by concept, map as many as possible to an existing data structure, but don't force matches where concepts don't align. For example, a product is not a web page, even if they have a few data concepts in common such as association, hierarchy, and content. For data statements that can't be mapped to existing data structures, create a new data model.

Using this approach you will produce a general data model. Additions to the data model are likely based on user interface designs, automated process outlines, and system interface designs. All of these are based on the business process stories and other requirements, so differences should be limited to minor details and not high level data concepts. Either way, data mappings for each of these artifacts need to be done and all details will be fleshed out.

Data model

The logical or conceptual aspects of a data model are best documented using data statements. The physical data model may be relational, object-oriented, or even document-oriented for structured documents such as JSON and XML.

While diagrams and descriptive documents may be helpful for doing data modeling and for users of the data model, the representation in data structure definitions (or other system usable artifacts) are usually sufficient. The creator has a technical background as do others who need to understand it. Less technical stakeholders will normally work with logical and conceptual data models represented by more easily understandable data statements.

The artifacts used to represent data models depend on the tools you will be using to implement the system. This may include XML entity definitions, SQL create table statements (DDL), class or interface code, XML schemas, or whatever your tools dictate.

Data mapping

Data mapping is a simple field level mapping between a design artifact and a physical data model. Mappings should be done for:

- user interfaces
- system interfaces
- automated processes

These are separate from the mappings done between data statements and the physical data model, which are an inherent part of data statements and the process to create a physical data model from them.

While data mappings can be represented in different forms, a plain table with a column for the name of the field in the design artifact and a column for the physical data element it maps to is simple and sufficient.

Many screens, reports, system interfaces, and so on involve more than one high level data structure (entity, table, class, document, etc). In these cases a little more information is needed to make sure things are implemented as desired. The relationship between the data structures needs to be defined in the mapping in terms of what you start with for the artifact and how you get from there to each other data structure that a field maps to.

For example when using relational entities or database tables you may have a screen with one or more ID values used to look up a record, or data for tabular output. Along with the actual field and the entity it is part of, describe the joins or additional queries needed to get from the main entity to that entity, and the key mappings needed to get from one entity to the next. When more complex queries are needed it is helpful to describe the query structure outside the data mapping table instead of trying to fit it inline.

Data mapping details make efforts easier for everyone involved with implementation. Using data mapping details developers know where to put data and where to get it from. QA engineers know where to look for data after it has been submitted to the system to validate that the right data gets to the right place, and for output that the data displayed matches what is persisted. System architects and senior developers, whether they worked on the data mapping, can review code and the behavior of the system against it.

Initial and test data

Initial data includes seed data that code relies on and is maintained with code, and configuration data that may change over time but at least represents the initial state planned for test and production deployment.

Test data demonstrates how the data model is used and acts as a further specification beyond the meta data of the data model. It is also useful for manual and automated tests written by developers and QA engineers.

The data should be maintained in files that can be easily loaded into the system in development, test, and (as applicable) production environments. These files will be manually created and maintained, so should be in some format that both humans and the system can work with such as XML, CSV, or SQL files.

The system will eventually run on migrated data, but during system design and implementation something is needed to demonstrate the intended model and use for testing. The manually created initial and test data establishes patterns that will be used for migrated data.

Automated process outline

Automated processes are based on activities in the business process story that the organization needs to handle automatically. The process may be triggered by a time-based event or by a user action, and the trigger should be described along with the process outline.

The outline itself is simply pseudo code describing what the system does. Make it as elaborate as you want, keeping in mind that if you go into too much detail you might as well write the code itself. Get the general idea and details important to the business documented, and let the developer do the rest.

System interface design

Just like user interfaces, interfaces to other systems need a design. If a specification is dictated by the other system the architect's job is limited to data mappings and mappings to internal APIs or services.

If the system interface is a new one to be offered by the system then the architect designs the format for data coming into the system and going out of it, and communication protocols and such for how the data is transported.

The technical details of system interfaces vary widely and with them the best way to represent those details.

If system representations of the interface (XML Schema, etc) are applicable include those in the design along with a description of document elements to accompany the mappings to internal system elements.

For new system interfaces this document will be used by developers working on this system and developers working on the other system(s). Make it sufficiently detailed and clear that a developer can build to it with minimal support. This is especially true if the system interface is offered to a number of partners or customers; more effort in documentation now will save effort in support and issue resolution later.

7. Implementation

Software development

The main artifacts developers use in implementation are designs, but it is helpful for developers to understand the business context for those designs and the business process story is the best for that. The short amount of time it takes to read through process stories provides developers with information about what the organization does to operate and saves immeasurable time in questions and misunderstanding throughout the development and QA processes.

One generally unacknowledged aspect of design and implementation is that all details must be decided on eventually. If they are not decided and detailed before a developer begins work it is implied that the developer should fill in the gaps in the implementation and wait for comments on the decisions. A goal of HEMP is to do sufficient requirements gathering and design to minimize this.

When building to detailed designs developers should not be free to make changes independently. The first review of the software will be done against the system design, and later on against the business requirements.

If a developer finds an issue with the design or requirements they should discuss it with the whoever worked on that artifact, such as the UI designer, system architect, or business analyst, and let the changes trickle through the process. When the design is changed then the developer can make corresponding changes to the implementation.

Implementation is where all the magic comes together. Depending on the tools used developers with different skill sets will be involved to produce quality software. If the requirements are correct and comprehensive, and the design is good and accurately based on the requirements, then an implementation based on the design will satisfy the needs of the organization to manage and automate its activities.

Quality assurance

Whichever tools and methods you use for testing, the basis of the tests is the same requirement and design artifacts that guide development.

High level and end-to-end test scripts, whether for manual or automated tests, are primarily based on business process stories. Details will come from design artifacts but the overall flow incorporates multiple actors and their actions and a process story is the best source for the flow.

Lower level tests such as unit and more granular integration tests are based on smaller parts of the system detailed in user interface designs, automated process outlines, system interface designs, and their corresponding data mappings.

Writing tests in advance is a good way to clarify and formalize specifications, but isn't as valuable when good requirements and designs are in place because the tests themselves would simply be based on them. For test-first development (writing tests before functional code), be they low-level or high-level tests, the ideas above apply.

Business implementation

Engagement of expert users and other stakeholders early in the process helps with acceptance but there is still work to be done to move an organization from one software system to another, or to get an organization going with its first system.

One way or another users of the new system need to learn how to use it. Some plan is needed for end-user documentation and/or training. Both of these can be based on business process stories where activities performed by actors within and outside an organization are documented. Just as it is easiest to build a system based on requirements structured by business process it is also easier for users to understand how to use the system when documentation is structured the same way.

If a gap/overlap analysis is done overlap descriptions make a good starting point for end-user documentation for business activities covered by an existing system. For business activities that led to design and implementation the UI designs and mappings to them from business process stories are a good basis for end-user documentation.

On the more technical side of things, production deployment of the system involves its own sort of design and execution. System performance and storage capacity can be planned for based on testing including data scale and user scale testing, but only fairly late in the development process. An infrastructure strategy can be laid out in advance but the exact hardware scale generally needs to wait for adequate scale testing. This is something a system architect and internal or outsourced IT would collaborate on.

Another major element of moving from one system to another is data migration. As mentioned before, data is a critical asset and resource for any organization: its information and meaning being all that matters after each activity is done.

The data model and mappings document the structure, meaning, and use of data in the new system, but specifications for the old system may be harder to come by. Support from people familiar with the old system may be necessary. The mapping of data between systems is another sort of data mapping, just like mappings between the data model and screens, system interfaces, and so on that are discussed in the technical design chapter. The same approach to documenting the mappings can be used.

Data migration for a comprehensive enterprise system is like writing hundreds of reports and requires significant effort for both data transformation scripts and testing of the completeness and correctness of the data in the new system. The migration effort should start when data mapping and modeling is completed so that once software development is complete the migrated data will be ready for testing and deployment with the software.

A large system requires significant effort to get all the pieces in place, but an experienced team will find the process much easier with the details available in the business requirement and system design artifacts used in HEMP.

Packaged Software and Marketing

One challenge with packaged software is communicating to prospective and current users what a system does and how things are done with it.

Business process stories are a useful tool to communicate what a system does in terms of the business activities it is designed to support. This helps prospective users understand what it was designed for in business terms they can understand. While the stories used as requirements for the software can be used as-is it is best to clean them up and test them with actual and prospective users before publishing them more widely.

For software that will be customized a story representing what is supported in the out-of-the-box system can be used as a starting point for requirements for a particular user organization and may be useful in early gap and overlap analysis to get an idea of how well a system might work for an organization.

Design artifacts can be used in similar ways to communicate how things are done. This is useful for prospective users to more quickly evaluate the system, and as mentioned elsewhere for current users to learn about the system.

Ongoing Development

Implementation and releasing a system into the world end the cycle started with analysis and design. The lifetime of a system can be very long and ongoing improvements may be done with many iterations of this cycle. The HEMP artifacts will be useful through every iteration and should by updated and leveraged to drive improvements over time.

During an initial development cycle there may be a large number of interrelated artifacts and the volume will only grow as the system progresses. The HEMP artifacts will also become more important for new expert users, analysts, designers, developers, testers, and others who get involved in later cycles.

Along with creating clear and well organized artifacts, it is helpful to have a good place to put them and keep them for as long as they are needed.

8. Tools and Systems

We have covered the various requirement and design artifacts, the roles involved with producing and consuming them, and the process for doing so. A question looms: where should all of this information go?

> Another benefit of the goal of keeping things simple is that the tools and systems required for managing HEMP artifacts can be simple as well.

There is no need for the common requirement and design software that has become so complex and expensive over decades of new methodologies with innumerable diagrams. These software packages often cost thousands of dollars per user and ultimately serve to increase complexity without material returns in efficiency or effectiveness.

The most useful tool for storage and organization of HEMP artifacts is a simple shared document repository like a wiki. To be effective there are a few features needed in such a document repository:

• hierarchy of documents
• sections within documents based on multiple levels of headings

- links within documents to sections or anchors in other documents
- attachments to documents for images and other supporting documents
- document revision management
  - history of changes and who made the change
  - view difference between any 2 revisions
  - unique revision number for each set of changes
- threaded comments on each document
- email notification for document updates
- easy online editing and immediate availability to others involved in the project
- support for multiple client platforms and operating systems, especially when outsourced teams are involved; a web-based solution is generally best

Simple web servers with HTML documents support the most important of these features, but there are many wiki systems that do a better job and are easier to use:

- Confluence from Atlassian is a good example of an effective commercial enterprise wiki
- Apache Bloodhound (based on Trac) is a good open source alternative that also includes project management
- HiveMind PM based on the Moqui Framework and Mantle Business Artifacts (these are open source projects that I am involved with) is another open source option with wiki, project management, request tracking, invoicing, etc

While HEMP minimizes the use of diagrams, some diagrams are still useful including wireframes, which are a specialized type of diagram. There are hosted or desktop tools such as Balsamiq and Gliffy that are sufficient for these, and desktop applications like OmniGraffle and Visio are useful as well. The choice for an application depends on team preferences and experience, especially for UI designers who will be the primary users of these tools.

Finally it is helpful to have some sort of project management system for tasks and requests. This software should also be an online system easily accessible by everyone involved with the project. This is very important for the actual software development, but also useful for managing the requirement gathering and design efforts.

Along with Confluence as an enterprise wiki, Atlassian offers a tool called Jira that can meet this need. The Apache Bloodhound and HiveMind PM applications are combined wiki and project manager applications designed just for these sorts of projects. There are dozens of other good open source and commercial options as well.

Other development tools such as a development environment (IDE) and code repository are critical for software projects. A single hosted code repository is vital, even if developers involved are spread across multiple internal and external organizations. Development tools are a little more flexible and will vary based on technologies used in the system architecture and developer preferences.

The code repository you decide on will also depend on developer preferences and experience. Subversion is a solid and flexible tool but lacks features for easy vender and other branch management that alternatives such as Git and Mercurial are designed to handle. This is especially important if you are extending an existing system, have source available for that system, and will be making changes to it as part of your project.

If the existing software is available on GitHub it is inexpensive to use a GitHub account to host your own code and "forks" of the existing software, and make them available to the teams working on the project.

While it is true that most developers are capable of deploying and managing these tools and applications it is a big distraction from the higher priority work they should be doing, so this is best handled as a separate role or outsourced altogether.

These are just some general recommendations and things to keep in mind when selecting tools for your project. There are so many good tools available, be they open source or commercial, and available as a hosted service or deployed and managed by your own IT personnel.

9. Case Studies

Now that you've slogged through all the details of HEMP you can enjoy some story time. Some of these case studies are failures that inspired HEMP, and others are examples of real world use.

Requirement and design distinction

The most spectacular failure I've seen to identify and distinguish requirements and designs was a multi-million-dollar project where a complex configurator driving both user interfaces and logic became a requirement. From the very beginning it was clear that this was a case of over-parameterization, but the parameterized (data-driven) architecture was specified as a "requirement".

I consulted on this project at the beginning of its 2 year life, then again around the middle, and again to do an evaluation closer to the end during renegotiation of the failed contract.

The real requirement was to build the system in such a way that it could be inexpensively maintained during its deployed life. Options presented to customers and associated pricing, dependencies, and so on would change as new products were introduced and offerings for products were changed over time.

The design was to fill this requirement by creating a data-driven configurator that drove nearly every aspect of the system. This was never evaluated as one of many possible designs to address the business requirement because it was presented from the beginning as THE big requirement for the system.

There are many ways to fail to distinguish between business requirements and system designs, but calling a system design a business requirement and not identifying the real requirements and then looking at alternative design options is by far the most potentially harmful.

How did the story end? If you have ever worked with such a system you'll have a good guess. The project went over budget and hit the end date without completing all functionality. The contract was renegotiated, lawsuits filed were settled, scope was reduced, delivery time was extended, and the initially simpler system was deployed and used in production.

About 5 years later a new team had taken over the system and was wondering how they could reduce the expense and effort of maintenance and change requests. It turned out this design was not only bad for the initial implementation but it also made ongoing maintenance and support for new products and offerings unreasonably expensive. This was so much the case that a new team was brought on to fix this issue, only to find out that doing so would require a nearly complete redesign and rewrite.

Even more interesting was a separate pilot project to build a similar system for the same company, but do so in a different way. This project was for a smaller division, but one that had similar requirements to the larger one. Instead of building a huge data-driven behemoth we designed to requirements and built to designs and did it fast enough to prove that the approach was not just measurably faster, but well over 10 times faster for maintenance and changes in offerings while requiring nearly zero upfront effort compared to the hundred-man-year behemoth that preceded it.

> It is difficult to predict the future and try to support it in advance. The expense is high and success rate low.

Stick with the requirements you've got and use agile architecture and development methods. Keep requirements and designs separated so that both the business and all others involved with the project know what the business needs and why the software is designed the way it is. With requirements and designs separated, question any outlandish or expensive designs where simpler ones may meet the requirements.

Analysis hysteria

One larger project included over 6 months of analysis efforts by a dozen analysts. The business itself was siloed enough that no one knew what all departments did and many used separate systems that did not communicate. The project was to consolidate dozens of systems into one that would supplement the core ERP system.

This is a difficult sort of project no matter how it is managed. To make it more difficult the analysis team included analysts with different levels of experience and familiarity with different artifacts and practices. There was no coordination to decide on a uniform set of artifacts or practices so it became an established practice for analysts to use whatever sort of artifact was desired to document requirements and designs.

The issue of requirements versus designs persisted throughout the project, but the most serious problem was the innumerable variety of diagrams and document structures. Analysts could not understand each others work, so knowledge only existed in the mind of each analyst, giving the benefit of the doubt that it was even clear to each analyst and they only failed to communicate it effectively.

Many experienced analysts have awareness of, or experience with, hundreds of different sorts of diagrams and other artifacts, and on top of that new diagram conventions are sometimes invented on the fly with no existing one meeting a certain need.

There are many business analysis books that discuss so many types of diagrams and documents that it is difficult to keep them straight, adding analysis complexity to business complexity. Very experienced analysts might be able to stick with standard diagrams and documents, and other experienced analysts might even understand their intended meaning. This doesn't help less experienced analysts, and leaves expert users, other business stakeholders, architects, and developers in the dark.

The result was an impressive pile of analysis artifacts that were unceremoniously thrown out in favor of designs based on discussion instead of on documented business requirements.

The lesson is to stick with a simple set of analysis and design artifacts that all involved agree on in advance and stick to in their work.

> Requirement and design artifacts should stand alone and not require assistance from another person to interpret.

Expert users, general stakeholders, and developers need to be able to understand them with minimal training. Artifacts that don't meet these objectives are doomed to be ignored or thrown out, defeating their intended purpose.

Dive into design

It's always tempting to skip requirements and dive into design. In many projects people don't understand the difference between requirements and designs so the business details gathered are a random mix of the two. In other projects there is push back on gathering requirements and a desire to skip to creating wireframes to get to software development quickly.

In one project the initial resistance to gathering requirements was based on existing documents from a failed project to address the same business needs. The documents were assumed to be adequate in spite of the failure of the previous project.

The existing documents were a confusing mix of requirements and designs. They were also found to be incomplete and incorrect so many times that they were eventually abandoned, but only after wasting hundreds of hours of work.

At this point the scope of the project was assumed to be known and well covered by the requirements gathered so far in spite of the inadequate documents. The decision was made to not start fresh with gathering pure requirements that designs could be based on, and to ensure that we really understood the full scope of business activities the system needed to support.

The result was a project that dragged on and on, blowing through round after round of estimates as new requirements were discovered every time designs were reviewed with the business. When initial acceptance testing of the implementation began the pace of requirement discovery increased substantially.

Acceptance testing is the point where you find out how good your requirements were. If they are known to be questionable the scope of the project is sure to mushroom when more business users start reviewing it. In this project that is exactly what happened.

Near the end the project team and corporate officers tried to cut off the flow of new requirements so the system could be deployed. Even this proved difficult and ultimately untenable because the business needed a certain set of functionality before it could migrate to the new system without changing business processes and operations.

The development side of the project went well, even though developers were spread across different consulting organizations and around the world. Part of the reason for this was good UI and technical designs following the patterns in HEMP. The analysis side of HEMP was proposed and used partly for one part of the business, but there was too much push back on analysis to use it in the rest.

The lesson is to make sure you have good requirements early in the process. If you get down the road a ways and find the flow of new requirements increasing instead of tapering off it means requirements are a problem.

It may be possible to complete the project with the same approach of increasing scope as needed based on iterations of business feedback. The risk is that the actual scope of the project is unknown and in a complex operation new requirements may continue to surface after it's too late to do anything about them without compromising the entire project.

Even if the system is deployed in production for use within the organization and replaces existing systems, confidence within the business and the project team will be low as long as issues and requirements continue to surface.

This can be solved by having part of the team or a new team do a fresh requirements gathering effort. This involves starting with no assumptions, reviewing all business activities, and documenting them as business process stories. Once that is done do a gap/overlap analysis with what has been built so far in the project (treating it as an existing system to follow the recommendations in Chapter 4, "Building on Existing Systems").

Once that is done you will have a better handle on the actual scope of the overall project and how much of it remains. A project plan can be established and tracked. An estimated delivery date can be more confidently set. An estimated budget can be set. If this is done well the flow of new requirements and issues surfacing should decrease dramatically and the confidence of all involved will improve.

HEMP ignited

No complex software project is perfect, but this one came pretty darn close.

The company was a funded startup with an innovative business model that required much automated customer interaction and integration with dozens of systems in other companies. An existing system was in place and working reasonably, but new feature development velocity was lower than desired and certain outsourced operations were to be brought in house and needed to be handled by the system.

The project started with a plan to use the HEMP process and artifacts, along with a proven open source ERP framework. The project team was a combination of internal development teams with some experience and outsourced teams that specialize in the existing system to be extended.

My personal involvement was in gathering and documenting all requirements, working with designers who did the actual UI designs, writing up technical designs and working with other experts on technical design, and then tasking out development work based on the designs and supporting around 20 developers.

The project was completed and deployed to replace existing systems and manage in-house operations in around 5 months. The new feature velocity after launch allowed the business to pursue new partnerships and offerings that had not been possible before.

The only wrinkle with such a tight timeline and with the majority of the team so focused on a frantic pace of development was inadequate time and resources planned for data migration. The result was a painful few days around the time of launch, a short delay in the planned launch schedule, and some data issues that had to be resolved after launch.

The new system involved business process changes, new security measures, operations changes to in-house major operations, two complex ecommerce sites, custom inventory and warehouse management for a specialized product, customer service changes and expansion, migration of a large amount of existing code and corresponding agreements for working with dozens of partners and service providers, and communication with hundreds of related businesses.

Part of the approach for handling the large scope and tight timeline was to identify business activities that were better known so that requirements and designs could be done quickly and development started, in this case within a couple of weeks of the start of the project. The requirements gathering and design for other parts of the project continued for around 4 months, until very close to the end. The project schedule made it necessary to run analysis, design, and implementation in parallel like this.

An initial business process story was written early on, but there were many changes to be made in the business and it took a long time to work through the complexities of these. This was a major concern throughout the project because the complete business activities were not finalized until close to the end of the project.

Following the HEMP process and using HEMP artifacts made it possible to handle the changes late in the project quickly and effectively. This included various long conversations on complex topics to establish the details of business activities. Once business process stories were updated the changes flowed quickly through to design and implementation. This allowed the organization to leverage the agility of the process and the underlying software during the initial development project as well as after it was deployed.

Important Lessons

Here is a summary of the lessons learned from these case studies. They are presented together here for easy reference and to make it easier to see how they are all interrelated.

Requirement and design distinction

- Clearly distinguish business requirements and system designs. Keep requirements about the business and designs about the system.
- Review requirements before designing the system to simplify and streamline wherever possible.
- Question any outlandish or expensive designs where simpler ones may meet the requirements.
- It is difficult to predict the future and try to support it in advance. The expense is high and success rate low. Stick with the requirements you've got and use agile architecture and development methods.

Analysis hysteria

- Stick with a simple set of analysis and design artifacts that all involved agree on in advance and stick to in their work.
- Requirement and design artifacts should stand alone and not require assistance from another person to interpret.

Dive into design

- Make sure you have good requirements early in the process. If you get down the road a ways and find the flow of new requirements increasing instead of tapering off it means requirements are a problem.
- If design and implementation are done without adequate business requirements they can be done later and the previous work can be evaluated with a gap/overlap analysis just like with any existing system.

HEMP ignited

- On large projects with short time frames you can do an initial pass on requirements for the entire business and then do detailed analysis, design, and implementation for various parts of the business in parallel and with different timelines.
- Following the HEMP process and using HEMP artifacts makes it possible to handle changes quickly and effectively, even late in a project.

Appendix: Examples

This chapter presents some simple examples to demonstrate the most important of the artifacts used in HEMP. For real systems and projects the actual artifacts will be much more complex and there will be a lot more of them, but their general nature and structure will be the same.

The business process story here is from the HiveMind PM open source project. It is related to the story of HEMP, but uses more generic actors and activities for the context of work planning and management.

The artifacts are presented here in a single section instead of spread throughout the book to make them easier to see and understand in the context of related artifacts.

Business process story

Group Manager reviews group tasks. Group Manager reviews tasks assigned to a group they manage including information such as task name, task type, description, priority, estimated work time, actual work time (work time so far), status, and due date. Group Manager assigns tasks to a member of their group, or delegates the task to another group.

Group Manager reviews tasks assigned to all members of their group. Group Manager may assign a task assigned to a Contributor in their group to another Contributor in their group, or delegate it to another group.

Group Manager and Contributors review outstanding tasks not associated with a milestone and the tasks associated with the next two milestones along with a total estimated time for all open tasks (deferred, omitted from design) and the working time available for the group in each milestone work period (deferred, omitted from design). Group Manager moves tasks between milestones and the unassociated set to plan work for the next milestone. (see the _Group Tasks by Milestone Screen_)

Group Manager and all Contributors assigned to a group review a task plan chart that shows for each Contributor the recent tasks worked on and projects future tasks for the next milestone (sorted by priority/ dependency, then by estimated time shortest first for equal priorities), with task working time determined by available calendar configured for each Contributor. Group Manager reassigns tasks to Contributors as needed to balance the work load for the coming milestone.

When Contributor has no tasks assigned to them needing attention or when wondering about other work to be done, Contributor reviews tasks assigned to a group they are a member of. Contributor accepts task assigned to a group they are in, making the task assigned to them.

Actor definition

Contributor - anyone who does work requested by a Client; may act as task assignee, request handler, and group member

Group Manager - person who manages a group of Contributors, may also be a Contributor

User experience story

Group Manager reviews requests and tasks assigned to the group, records comments as needed, and assigns them to a Contributor in the group or if required expertise or working time is not available in the group then delegates to another group.

If milestones (sprints, etc) are used Group Manager works with group members to plan upcoming work by associating tasks with milestones, moving tasks between milestones or un-associating deferred tasks. Group Manager reviews upcoming schedule and reassigns requests and tasks between group members to balance work load.

Group Manager supports group members to get questions answered, manage expectations, adjust schedule and requirements, and so on. Group Manager works with other Group Managers to coordinate within the larger project.

Group Manager works with Account Manager and Client Representative to review incoming requests, report on status and estimates of requests and tasks, establish priorities, and so on.

Data statement

These data statements are examples based on the business process story. The data mappings are in parenthesis following each statement.

Group Manager is a system user. (*UserAccount*)

Contributor is a system user. (*UserAccount*)

Group Manager manages a Contributor Group. (*PartyRelationship* with *relationshipTypeEnumId = Manager*)

Contributor Group has one or more Group Members. (*PartyRelationship* with *relationshipTypeEnumId = Member*)

Contributor Group is an Organization. (*Party* of type *Organization*)

Group Member is a Contributor. (No mapping needed)

Group Manager is a Person. (*Party* of type *Person*)

Contributor is a Person. (*Party* of type *Person*)

Task is a low-level work effort. (*WorkEffort* with *workEffortTypeEnumId = Task*)

Task can be assigned to Contributor Group. (*WorkEffortParty*)

Task can be assigned to Contributor. (*WorkEffortParty*)

Task has Contributor and Group assignment history. (*WorkEffortParty via fromDate and thruDate*)

Task can be associated with Milestone.
(*WorkEffortAssoc* with *workEffortAssocTypeEnumId* = *Milestone*)

Project is a high-level work effort. (*WorkEffort* with *workEffortTypeEnumId* = *Project*)

Project has one or more Milestones. (*WorkEffortAssoc* with *workEffortAssocTypeEnumId* = *Milestone*)

Milestone is a work effort. (*WorkEffort* with *workEffortTypeEnumId* = *Milestone*)

Task has an estimated work time and actual work time. (*WorkEffort.estimatedWorkTime*, *WorkEffort.actualWorkTime*)

Task has a priority and due date. (*WorkEffort.priority*, *WorkEffort.estimatedCompletionDate*)

Task has a status. (*WorkEffort.statusId*)

Task has a name and description. (*WorkEffort.workEffortName*, *WorkEffort.description*)

Task has a type/purpose. (*WorkEffort.purposeEnumId*)

Task is part of a Project. (Task WorkEffort.rootWorkEffortId = Project workEffortId)

Task has one or more sub-tasks. (Sub-task WorkEffort.parentWorkEffortId = Task workEffortId)

Data model

This is a brief outline of a physical data model for example purposes. The actual representation would be more comprehensive and in whatever form is used for the development tools you are using (SQL DDL, XML entity definition, XSD, etc).

The data model here is an excerpt from the Universal Data Model (UDM) in the Mantle Business Artifacts project. It includes only the entities and fields relevant to this example.

- UserAccount
  - userAccountId (pk)
  - username
  - password
  - partyId (fk)
- Party
  - partyId (pk)
  - partyTypeEnumId (fk)
    - Person
    - Organization
- Person
  - partyId (pk)
  - firstName
  - lastName
- Organization
  - partyId (pk)
  - organizationName
- PartyRelationship
  - partyId (pk, fk)
  - toPartyId (pk, fk)
  - relationshipTypeEnumId (pk, fk)
    - Manager
    - Member
- WorkEffort
  - workEffortId (pk)
  - workEffortTypeEnumId (fk)
    - Project

- Milestone
- Task
- purposeEnumId
  - For Task type
    - New Feature
    - Improvement
    - Bug
- parentWorkEffortId (fk)
- rootWorkEffortId (fk)
- workEffortName
- description
- estimatedWorkTime
- actualWorkTime
- statusId
  - In Planning
  - Approved
  - In Progress
  - Complete
  - Closed
  - On Hold
  - Cancelled
- priority
- estimatedStartDate
- estimatedCompletionDate
- WorkEffortParty
  - workEffortId (pk, fk)
  - partyId (pk, fk)
  - fromDate (pk)
  - thruDate
- WorkEffortAssoc
  - workEffortId (pk, fk)
  - toWorkEffortId (pk, fk)
  - workEffortAssocTypeEnumId (pk, fk)
    - Milestone

- fromDate (pk)
- thruDate

Screen outline

Group Tasks by Milestone Screen

- Top Section
  - Milestone and Group Form
    - Project drop-down
      - includes all projects associated with current user
      - order by project start date
      - defaults to first project in the list
    - Milestone drop-down
      - based on project selected shows all milestones in the project
      - defaults to the next milestone (earliest milestone start date in the future)
    - Group drop-down
      - includes all groups associated with the selected project
    - "Select" button
- Main Section
  - initially hidden, displays after Milestone and Group Form is submitted
  - Split into three columns
    - Left
      - "Unassociated" heading
      - List all tasks in current project not associated with any milestone, sorted by priority ascending (lowest number highest priority)
    - Middle

- "Selected Milestone - ${selected milestone name}" heading
- Milestone start and end dates
- list all tasks in the current milestone, sorted by priority ascending
- Right
  - "Next Milestone - ${next milestone name}" heading
  - Milestone start and end dates
  - list all tasks in the milestone after the current milestone (first start date after the start date of the selected milestone), sorted by priority ascending
- For each task in each column
  - Task ID (with link to Task Detail page)
  - Task Name
  - Task Type
  - Priority
  - Due Date
  - Estimated Work Time
  - Actual Work Time (based on time entries)
  - Status
  - Assigned to drop-down
    - include all Contributor Groups assigned to project and Contributors assigned to the selected Group
    - default to the currently assigned Contributor or Contributor Group
    - submit automatically in background on change of selection
  - Move buttons
    - "Disassociate", "${selected milestone name}", and "${next milestone name}"

- show the two buttons associated with the other two columns (ie don't show button for current column)
- when clicked associate the task with the corresponding column and update the screen (including expiring the association to put it in the left column if Disassociate button is clicked)

Wireframe

Group Tasks by Milestone Screen

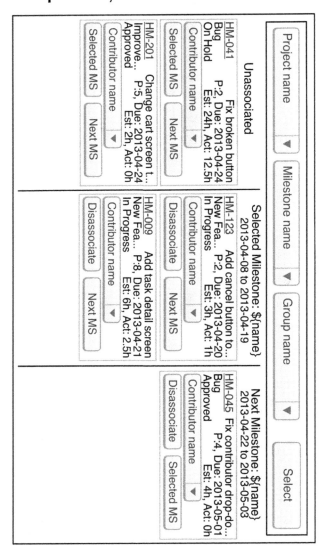

Screen data mapping

Group Tasks by Milestone Screen

Milestone and Group Form	
Project drop-down options	join of WorkEffort and WorkEffortParty on workEffortId where WorkEffort. workEffortTypeEnumId = Project AND WorkEffortParty.partyId is UserAccount.partyId of logged in user show WorkEffort. workEffortName
Milestone drop-down options	WorkEffort where rootWorkEffortId = project workEffortId AND workEffortTypeEnumId = Milestone
Group drop-down options	join of WorkEffortParty and Organization on partyId where WEP. workEffortId = project workEffortId (inner join so will only get Organizations back) show Organization. organizationName
Main Columns	

Left columns tasks	WorkEffort where rootWorkEffortId = project workEffortId AND no WorkEffortAssoc records exist with workEffortAssocTypeEnumId = Milestone AND active fromDate/thruDate
Middle and right column tasks	based on workEffortId of selected milestone for middle column, and of the next milestone by estimatedStartDate for the right column: join of WorkEffortAssoc and WorkEffort on WEA.toWorkEffortId = WE.workEffortId where WEA.workEffort = milestone workEffortId AND WEA. workEffortAssocTypeEnumId = Milestone WE is the task WorkEffort
Middle and right column milestone names	WorkEffort.workEffortName for milestone workEffortId
Middle and right column start and end dates	WorkEffort.estimatedStartDate and WorkEffort. estimatedCompletionDate for milestone workEffortId

Task Detail	Look up WorkEffort record using task workEffortId
Task ID	WorkEffort.workEffortId
Task Name	WorkEffort.workEffortName
Task Type	Enumeration.description where enumId = WorkEffort.purposeEnumId
Priority	WorkEffort.priority
Due Date	WorkEffort. estimatedCompletionDate
Estimated Work Time	WorkEffort.estimatedWorkTime
Actual Work Time	WorkEffort.actualWorkTime
Status	StatusItem.description where statusId = WorkEffort.statusId

Assigned to drop-down options	<u>Groups</u>: join of WorkEffortParty and Organization on partyId where WEP.workEffortId = project workEffortId (inner join so will only get Organizations back) show ORG.organizationName, key on ORG.partyId <u>Contributors</u>: join of PartyRelationship and Person on PR.toPartyId = PER.partyId where PR.partyId = selected group partyId AND PR. relationshipTypeEnumId = Member show PER.firstName and PER.lastName, key on PER.partyId
Assigned to drop-down current	WorkEffortParty where workEffortId is task workEffortId AND filter by fromDate/thruDate, use partyId for selected key